'KELWAY'S G

The story of a pioneering Somerset nursery

Janet Seaton

Kelways Heritage Series No.1

About the author

Janet Seaton worked at the House of Commons Library for twenty years and established the new Scottish Parliament's research and information service. Her publications include *Facts about the British Prime Ministers* (1995) and *Political London* (2000). She is a member of the Royal Horticultural Society and the Society of Genealogists, and was awarded an OBE in 2008. She lives in Langport, Somerset with a husband and two cats.

Published in Great Britain in 2011 by Picts Hill Publishing an imprint of Even Handed Licensing Limited.

ISBN **978-1-904496-07-6**

Picts Hill Publishing
Even Handed Licensing Limited
PO Box 93
Langport
TA10 1AP

CONTENTS

*Wherever a love of gardening and horticulture
generally exists, the name of Kelway is a
household word.*
(*The Garden,* 16 Oct 1909, p.503)

Preface

I knew the Kelways name through going to Chelsea Flower Shows when I lived in London. Then, years later, when I moved to Langport, I was intrigued to find that they were still there, just up the road. As soon as I realised that 2011 was their 160th anniversary, and discovered that nobody had published a history of the nursery, I was determined to tell their story.

James Kelway arrived in Huish Episcopi, Langport's neighbouring parish, in 1851. Within fifty years both he and the nursery that still bears his name had achieved a world wide reputation. They became best known for gladioli and peonies: 'Kelway's Glorious' was their most successful peony introduction.

The Kelway family and Kelways Nursery are an integral part of the landscape and history of this part of Somerset, but they also made their mark in the world of horticulture. It's high time their achievements were celebrated.

Acknowledgements

The present owners of Kelways have supported me throughout this project, and have given me full access to their records, for which I am extremely grateful.

I would also like to thank the staff of the RHS Lindley Library, and the Somerset Heritage Centre, as well as the many individuals who have provided information and advice.

In particular I'd like to thank Dave Root, Andy Martin, Norman Parfitt, David Kelway, Jo Stradling, Andrew Lee and my husband Barry Winetrobe.

Illustrations
All images are copyright Kelways Plants Ltd except for the portrait of William Kelway on p.15, which is reproduced with permission of the Estate of Dame Laura Knight DBE RA 2011. The front cover shows the peony 'Kelway's Glorious'. On the back cover is a recent photograph of the Old Kelways buildings, Somerton Road, Langport.

Spelling
When referring to the nursery business I have used both Kelway's and Kelways, depending on context. Peony is spelled without the 'a' unless it is being quoted, or when Latin plant names are used.

Sources
Most of the information is extracted from Kelways' catalogues and records, or other primary sources, but for brevity and ease of reading, references and footnotes have not been included.

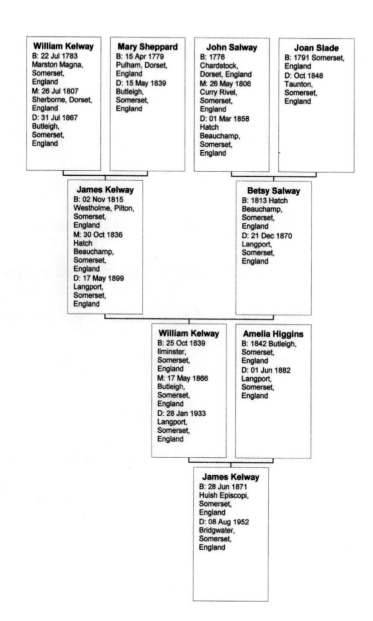

William Kelway
B: 22 Jul 1783
Marston Magna,
Somerset,
England
M: 26 Jul 1807
Sherborne, Dorset,
England
D: 31 Jul 1867
Butleigh,
Somerset,
England

Mary Sheppard
B: 15 Apr 1779
Pulham, Dorset,
England
D: 15 May 1839
Butleigh,
Somerset,
England

John Salway
B: 1776
Chardstock,
Dorset, England
M: 26 May 1806
Curry Rivel,
Somerset,
England
D: 01 Mar 1858
Hatch
Beauchamp,
Somerset,
England

Joan Slade
B: 1791 Somerset,
England
D: Oct 1848
Taunton,
Somerset,
England

James Kelway
B: 02 Nov 1815
Westholme, Pilton,
Somerset,
England
M: 30 Oct 1836
Hatch
Beauchamp,
Somerset,
England
D: 17 May 1899
Langport,
Somerset,
England

Betsy Salway
B: 1813 Hatch
Beauchamp,
Somerset,
England
D: 21 Dec 1870
Langport,
Somerset,
England

William Kelway
B: 25 Oct 1839
Ilminster,
Somerset,
England
M: 17 May 1866
Butleigh,
Somerset,
England
D: 28 Jan 1933
Langport,
Somerset,
England

Amelia Higgins
B: 1842 Butleigh,
Somerset,
England
D: 01 Jun 1882
Langport,
Somerset,
England

James Kelway
B: 28 Jun 1871
Huish Episcopi,
Somerset,
England
D: 08 Aug 1952
Bridgwater,
Somerset,
England

The Kelways who shaped the nursery

8

Chapter 1
The Kelway family

One of the significant features of the Kelway family is its longevity. James was 83 when he died; his father William lived to the age of 84; his son William lived to 94 and was Langport's oldest inhabitant when he died. That William's son, also James, died at the age of 81. Some have attributed this to the gardening way of life.

William Kelway (1783-1867), James's father
The first William was born in Marston Magna, Somerset, on 22 July 1783. When his second son James was born, he was Head Gardener to Major Thomas Clerk of Westholme House, near Shepton Mallet. Later he worked at Hatch Court, and then for John Tudway, who was MP for Wells. After Tudway's retirement, he took up the post of gardener to the Neville-Grenvilles at Butleigh Court, where he remained until he retired. He died in Butleigh and is buried with his second wife, Jane, in Butleigh churchyard.

James Kelway (1815-1899)
James Kelway was born on 2 November 1815 in the parish of Westholme, Somerset. He left school at 13 and spent the next five years training as a gardener under his father's supervision. After only two years he began to enter flower shows, and success at a show in Glastonbury in 1830 seems to have given him a taste for competition. More importantly, this was where he first saw the brightly coloured red and yellow *Gladiolus psittacinus* that sparked his interest in gladioli.

At the age of 18, James was taken on by John Lee Lee as the Head Gardener at Dillington House, near Ilminster, Somerset. Once the home of the 18th century Prime Minister, Lord North, it had been inherited by the Lee family, and the estate was undergoing a complete refurbishment.

James Kelway, founder of the nursery

According to family tradition, James used to write notes on the back of the potting shed doors. As well as simple jottings, these notes also recorded the arrival of swallows, and the first cuckoo of spring. None of the dated notes are old enough to be from his time in the gardens, but others may have been in his handwriting. Although two of the potting sheds or 'bothies' are still there, the original doors, unfortunately for posterity, have been replaced.

James had a small staff, and transformed the layout of the garden during the 17 years that he worked there. A landscape survey in 2005 described his achievement in the gardens as 'the greatest development possibly since the 1620s', and subsequent proposals for restoration recommended that, 'A bed on either side of the central axis in the southern area should be planted each year with colourful annuals reflecting Kelway's pioneering horticulture'. Some time around 1850, James bought just over an acre of land in Huish Episcopi from a James Isaacs, of Langport Eastover. The land included a small house and a greenhouse, and may have already been in use as a smallholding. At any rate his father must have helped him to establish his nursery business, as it is William who is recorded in the 1851 census as living at Wearne, in Huish Episcopi, with his second wife Jane and their grandson William Tutton. James is recorded as a gardener, still living at Ashwill, Ilminster.

Kelways Nursery was founded, according to their own tradition, on May Day, 1851. In 1856, in his first-known advertisement in the local press, James described himself as 'nurseryman, seedsman and florist'.

He was renowned for his capacity for hard work. His daily routine saw him rising at 6 am, having no more than half an hour for breakfast and an hour for lunch, and finishing work at 6pm. He was usually the first to arrive and the last to leave, six days a week.

James became a founding member and honorary secretary of the Wells Floral and Horticultural Society, which held its first show in August 1860. The only other shows in the area at that time were at Bath and Langport. He himself exhibited at the Wells show a model garden which included a cascade and a fountain. Despite poor weather, the show was judged to have been a success.

In 1867 he moved into Gladioli Villa, a house he had built in the grounds of the nursery and named after his favourite flower. It is now called Wearne Lodge, but the Kelway coat of arms can still be seen on the weathervane. His wife Betsy died in December 1870, and he had a stained glass window erected to her memory in the church where he was a churchwarden, St Mary's, Huish Episcopi.

Two years later he married Charlotte Warren, of Royston, in Hertfordshire, whose father was a printer. The earliest extant Kelway's catalogue, the Spring Catalogue for 1872, was printed by 'The Royston Press: John Warren'.

In 1887 Frank Miles was commissioned to paint his portrait, and spent a month with him at his home. Miles described him as a 'grand old gardener: seventy-one, keen of eye, and quick of understanding, white on head and chin and cheek'.

In 1890 James received two honours of which he must have been very proud. William Robinson, editor of *The Garden*, and a leading horticulturist, dedicated the 1890 volume of *The Garden* to him 'in acknowledgement of his work among garden flowers'. In that same year he was invited by the Royal Horticultural Society (RHS) to deliver a lecture on the subject of the cultivation of gladioli, which he did on 9 September.

When he died in 1899, the obituaries in the horticultural press were long and respectful. The *Gardeners' Magazine* stated, 'With perfect justification, therefore, was the late Mr.

Kelway described some years since as "one of the great horticultural lights of the Victorian era"'. *The Garden* commented, 'We believe we fall even short of the actual truth when we say that this week his loss will be mentioned with regret in every town and district in England, so well was his name or person known by amateur and professional devotees of horticulture'. The *Gardeners' Chronicle* agreed, 'he has closed his active career, carrying with him to his grave the regrets, not only of a wide circle of friends and acquaintances, but also with those of the extensive district throughout which he was so widely known.'

William Kelway (1839-1933), James' son
James' son William and his grandson James followed him into the nursery business. William had inherited his father's love of plant breeding. 'I have spared no effort spending all my spare moments for half a century in the cross-fertilisation of flowers,' he wrote in 1909.

He lived at Brooklands, a house which he had built of the distinctive local white lias stone. It stands near the site of the Battle of Langport, the penultimate battle of the English Civil War, fought on 10 July 1645, and from time to time he dug cannonballs out of the ground. After his death in 1933, the house was bought by Somerset County Council and became a remand home for many years. Now called Bartletts Elm, it is the site of a housing development.

William was married twice. His first wife, Amelia Higgins, died in 1882. His second wife, Sara Stewart, was Scottish, and they were married in Glasgow on 9 May 1891. On the day of that wedding, church bells were rung in Langport and Huish Episcopi in their honour. Prior to leaving home for Scotland, 50 to 60 of Kelways' staff had given him a wedding present with an address of congratulations and good wishes for his future happiness. It was to be several months before they saw him again, since his honeymoon took him on an extensive tour of the United States and Canada. However, he did promise that they would all be invited to a supper to celebrate his return in July!

William Kelway in 1901

He was a County Councillor for 21 years. For many elections he was returned unopposed, although at his first attempt in 1892, to his evident annoyance, he and his 'brother ratepayers' were put to the expense of a contest. He claimed to be 'the labourer's friend' and pledged to keep the rates down. But, although he printed campaign posters which boasted lists of prominent supporters, he had not previously been active in public life, and did not hold any public meetings. When he lost to the much better known J T Knight by 86 votes, the press attributed his defeat in part to his passive campaigning.

William Kelway, framed in delphiniums, painted by Harold Knight.

15

When he died in 1933 at the age of 94, he was described as Langport's 'Grand Old Man', being the oldest inhabitant. His obituary in the local newspaper remarked, 'Largely due to his acumen and assiduity Kelway's became famous, especially for gladioli, paeonies and delphiniums, and the firm established a world wide trade.'

William and James Kelway and family, photographed for Country Life in 1900

James Kelway (1871-1952), James's grandson

The second James was William's eldest son, the only surviving son from his first marriage, but he had two half brothers, Kenneth and Ian.

James Kelway in 1900

He became a partner in the family business in 1905 and was in sole charge after his father retired in 1925. He was Vice-President of the British Gladiolus Society, and was also an enthusiastic peony breeder. Towards the end of his life he wrote a book about them, *Garden paeonies*, which was published after his death. In the final sentence he summed up his obsession, 'My conclusion must be that in the paeony one has consummate loveliness and a perennial joy in return for a minimum of expenditure in money and labour.'

James Kelway married Ella Stubbs, the only daughter of the vicar of the local church, St Mary's, Huish Episcopi, in a stylish ceremony on a beautiful sunny day in September 1896. Flowers were very much the theme of the occasion, with the churchyard wall festooned with sprigs of gladioli and evergreens, and even a floral arch spanning the road where the couple had to cross from the Vicarage to the Church. A red cloth was laid from the Vicarage to the altar, and the couple passed through a guard of honour provided by H Company, 2nd Volunteer Battalion, Prince Albert's Somerset Light Infantry, in which James was a lieutenant. The list of wedding presents recorded in the local newspaper was prodigious and varied, ranging from a freehold property to a pickle fork. After their return from honeymoon James and his wife moved into Wearne Wyche, a large house about half a mile from the nursery.

Like his father, James played an active part in local life. When he died in 1952, he left a wife, son and four daughters.

Coat of arms
The Kelways were interested in their family history, and used a coat of arms on their catalogues.

The arms of Kelway are described in *Burke's General Armory* (1884) as 'Ar (*silver*), two thigh bones in saltire sa (*black*), between four pears or (*gold*), a bordure engr. of the second (*black*).' An earlier work suggests that there were sometimes glaziers' snippers or irons instead of bones.

The Kelway family seems to have been associated with glazing, probably at the time of the building of Sherborne Abbey in Dorset. The pear is thought to be derived from the

French 'Caillou' or Burgundy pear which was commonly planted in England before the 19th century. The motto 'dulcius ex asperis' means 'sweeter after difficulties'.

Quarterings are used to display descent from other families, and this particular one seems to refer to Ellis and Cammel. It bears a striking similarity to the arms held by William Kellaway, of Whiteparish, Wiltshire in 1565, but there is no proven link between the nursery Kelways and the Wiltshire Kellaways.

Coat of arms on the cover of the 1879/80 gladiolus catalogue

Memorials
The church of St Mary the Virgin (St Mary's), Huish Episcopi, has many memorials dedicated to members of the Kelway family, both inside the church and in the churchyard.

Three of the stained glass windows relate to Kelways. James had dedicated one to his first wife, Betsy, and a second was erected in memory of his second wife,

Charlotte, after her death in 1913. However, the most spectacular is in the south aisle, depicting the nativity, which was designed by the noted artist Sir Edward Burne-Jones and erected in 1899 in memory of the first James Kelway. William presented a brass eagle lectern dedicated to the memory of his wife Amelia.

At the corner of the churchyard facing the main road stands an imposing white marble obelisk in memory of the Kelway family. Several generations are buried and remembered there. Kelways Nursery has planted peonies with appropriate names as a mark of respect to the family.

A catalogue of 1890 advertising their Paris Gold Medal

Chapter 2
The Kelways' management of the nursery

James Kelway once said, 'Nothing like land, it can't run away'. He started the nursery with less than two acres of land, and by the time he died in 1899 it covered 200 acres which they owned, plus many more acres leased from farmers in order to grow seed crops for them.

The golden years

The skill and hard work of James and his son William saw the nursery go from strength to strength during the 19th century. James lost no time in making his nursery's mark at local flower shows, winning a Silver Cup for his dahlias at the Wellington Flower Show in 1858 and 1859, and also at the first ever Langport Flower Show in 1859.

At the Central Somerset Flower Show in 1860 Kelways won their first award for gladioli. For the next 50 years the gladiolus became their mainstay. In 1914 they were able to claim that 'The history of the gladiolus since 1851 is co-extensive with, and almost entirely a part of, the history of the firm of Kelway & Son.'

In 1864 William became a partner, and the business became Kelway & Son. William was not well liked by those who worked for him. One employee remembered William as a strict man who used to observe his workers through a small spy-hole cut into an umbrella, which he carried raised in front of him. They were forbidden to whistle, and if he caught them, they were fined sixpence. If they met him in the street, even ladies had to step off the pavement to let him pass. The Kelways buildings, with the distinctive Kelway's arch, were probably constructed during the 1870s. The three and four storey warehouses had first and second storey walkways between them. At the front of the building a bell was installed which was rung night and morning in a tradition that lasted over 100 years. There was a central lift and pulley system to get sacks of seeds up to the upper storeys, and racks and pigeon holes to store them. A series of bowls and scoops with long and short handles were designed for the different seeds.

Kelway's arch and buildings, Somerton Road, Langport

In 1881 William was described in the census return as a nursery and seed merchant employing 30 men, 10 boys and 10 women on 140 acres of land.

James's chief recreation was his visits to Paris for the French Exhibitions. Much to their delight, at the exhibition in 1889 Kelways were awarded a Gold Medal 'for general excellence of gladiolus and other exhibits'.

Kelways also exhibited at shows in the USA, where other flowers were more successful. We can only speculate on the logistics of how this was achieved. At the Columbian Exhibition in Chicago in 1893 they received a Special Award, Medal and Diploma for *Primula sinensis* Kelway's Perfect Model red.

At the turn of the century Kelways could claim to be a business operating on a world-wide scale. 'Kelway's export trade to India, America, Canada, Australia, South Africa, New Zealand, China, Japan, South America, France, Germany, Russia, Austria, Scandinavia, Denmark, Netherlands, and other colonies, dependencies and foreign countries is extensive and increasing in volume year by year...' Testimonials from customers in many of these countries were reprinted year after year as evidence of this success. No doubt their appearance at major horticultural shows abroad raised their international profile.

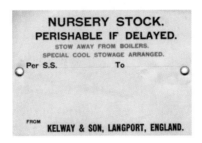

Label for dispatch by sea

At St Louis in 1904, at a major exhibition held alongside the third Olympic Games, they evidently caused quite a stir,

Gold Medal certificate, St Louis 1904

winning gold for a collection that included Kelway's cultivars

23

of calceolaria, cineraria, cyclamen, delphiniums, gaillardia, gladioli, gloxinia, *Primula Sinensis* and *Pyrethrum roseum*.

In 1915 they won a Medal of Honour for 'the best Collection of Flowering Annuals' at the Panama-Pacific Exhibition in San Francisco. They also exhibited regularly at the Massachusetts Horticultural Society Show, where they presented medals.

At the beginning of the 20th century, however, the nursery was evidently feeling the cold draught of competition. Their 1904 *Manual of horticulture* stressed the advantages they had by being based in the rural countryside.

> 'Our seeds, grown by ourselves without the great additional expense entailed by city warehouses, offices and town labour, are for these reasons reliable as well as inexpensive.'

They were also taking advantage of the rise in railway travel. Langport had had a railway station since 1853, but it was a branch line, and on the Taunton side of Great Bow Bridge, some distance from the nursery. A new Great Western Railway line connected Langport directly to London when Langport East Station opened in 1906. This line ran through the land occupied by Kelways Nursery, and they offered special delivery rates for those who used the train.

Even before Langport East Station was opened, they were able to say, with understandable hyperbole, 'Railway rates have been so greatly reduced recently that distance is annihilated, and Kelway & Son are now for all practical purposes in the same town as their customers.'

Parcels being loaded up for dispatch by rail

The scale of their operations was impressive. The nursery had been described as 'a city set on a hill'. In 1910 there was the home nursery; England's Fields (a big addition to the original ground on which the company was started); Barrymore Fields; the Allotments; 2 great seed stores – four-storied buildings; the gladioli and bulb store. Nursery staff numbered well over 100, plus those employed on the seed farms. The *Gardeners' Magazine* reported, 'Everywhere it was apparent that here is a vast, well organised business that is of immense importance to the immediate neighbourhood, as well as to British horticulture.' In 1912 the average wage for a Kelway employee working a six day week was 14/- (about £60 today).

They employed three 'travellers' who represented them in different parts of the country: one for the South and West of England, South Wales and London; one for 'England between Tyne and Thames', and one to cover Ireland, Scotland and the Borders, and North Wales.

Seed and bulb warehouses, with greenhouses below

But their troubles were clearly on the increase. There was an unfortunate row in Scotland in 1912 about the poor germination of carrots, which cost them dear both in bad publicity and in paying compensation to disgruntled growers.

By 1913 Kelways had decided to concentrate exclusively on the wholesale seed market. The cover of their seed catalogue for 1914 boasted, 'strains selected on our 300 acre farm-nursery in sunny Somerset'. However, the storm clouds of war and economic recession were gathering on the horizon.

Kelways in the First World War

The First World War came as something of a shock to the seed and nursery trade. It was arguably the beginning of the end of the nursery's steady expansion over the previous 60 years. Grand estates and large gardens declined as gardeners went off to war, and Kelways were forced to switch their focus from flowers to agriculture, and specifically food production.

As employers they combined a social conscience with fierce

and open patriotism. A slip for insertion into their catalogues for 1914 bore the heading, 'The prevention of distress is better than its relief, and employment is better than charity', and went on to promise to send 5% of the value of all orders received before Christmas to wartime charities.

They were also proud of staff who had joined up to fight for their country. In 1915 they published *Kelways Roll of Honour*, which listed the names of 45 'Kelwayans' (employees who joined the British army or navy direct from Kelway & Son) and 60 'Old Kelwayans' (people who were employed at Kelways before August 1914 and who were now serving in the armed forces).

Nevertheless, as the war dragged on, it became increasingly difficult to operate without skilled labour. In the 1900s they had employed just over a hundred staff, but the outbreak of war led to a drastic reduction, with fewer than 40 employed by July 1917. James regularly complained about the impact of wartime regulations on what he regarded as a vital business, especially in the transfer of skilled labour to the forces and other war work. He ended one letter to *The Times* with a plea for wholesale seed growers and merchants to be treated 'as if they were making munitions of war, as indeed they are'.

They did their best to sustain their market position, appealing to patriotic sentiment whenever they could. They even invented an ingeniously themed border, the Allies' Colour Border, offered under the name of 'Triple Entente'.

In 1914 and 1916 they won orders to supply seeds to the US government. In 1916 forty firms bid for a share in the contract, and Kelways were one of only two non-US firms who were successful, the other being Vilmorin, of Paris. The order was placed by the Congressional Seed Distribution

Office, whose remit was to provide seeds to farmers via their Congressional representatives. Originally designed to encourage pioneer farmers to try new varieties of plants, this scheme, in operation since the mid 1850s, had degenerated into a thinly veiled means of helping Congressmen to buy favour with the farming community in their districts. Doubtless unaware of its controversial political overtones, Kelways were delighted to secure the business at such a difficult time.

As the end of the war drew near, they lost no opportunity to once again market their speciality, the gladiolus. Its name derives from 'gladius', Latin for sword, so they advertised it as 'the Soldier's Flower', the ideal flower 'to greet our soldiers and sailors on their return in the autumn'.

Despite their best efforts, however, the golden days of exuberant mass plantings of flower borders and lavish expenditure on gardens in general were numbered.

The struggle for survival
The wartime years had taken their toll on the land itself. The soil was exhausted, and couch grass had taken hold in many areas. Infestations of insects were also causing real problems. The turnip flea beetle and the pygmy mangold beetle could decimate their crops, with almost no pesticides available to control them. Restoring the nursery to its former glory was an uphill battle.

Although the post war economic situation was gloomy, Kelways' reputation was still high. 'In the floral world 'Progress' must always be the watchword. Messrs Kelway know it, act up to it, and their fame and reputation are still in the ascendant'. Unfortunately for them, fame and reputation did not fill their order books.

At the outset of war the number of gardens in Somerset large enough to employ a full time gardener was 137, but ten years later it had fallen by a third, never to recover. In 1922 Kelways were forced to offer 25% off their prices for named varieties of peonies and delphiniums, as well as Michaelmas daisies, dahlias, gaillardias, hybrid lupins, phloxes, pyrethrums and gladioli.

At the same time wages were rising. The annual wage bill for the year to July 1920 came to £6,942, and they were again employing close to 100 staff. These figures gradually reduced over the next few years as the nursery business declined in common with the rest of the economy. The business was in trouble, and little was spent on the maintenance and upkeep of the nursery buildings.

The partnership between William and James Kelway was dissolved by mutual consent on 31 December 1924, leaving James in sole control of the company, which became known as Kelways Limited. In the preface to their *Manual of horticulture* for 1926 he reflected on the company's situation in terms which revealed the damaging after-effects of the war.

> 'At the opening of the first year of the Peace, as distinguished from the period since the War which so aptly has been termed Purgatory, we may be allowed a few moments in which to review the past as it has affected Horticulture and ourselves … – we all know the grievous tale of the distressing years of War which destroyed utterly so many human schemes, large or small, fine or mean. For a while the hill of achievement was obscured…'

Sadly for James Kelway, grandson of the founder of the nursery, the hill of achievement proved too steep, and within

8 years he was facing bankruptcy. It was the beginning of the end of the family's ownership of the business.

English seed crops featured in their shop window

On 16 January 1933 James Kelway was forced to apply for the company's winding up. When he appeared at Yeovil Bankruptcy Court in February 1933, it was a sorry tale that he had to tell. He explained that when he took over the firm, many of the buildings were in need of repair. He himself had only taken £1,000 per year in salary, which he thought was reasonable. He had not taken a holiday for the past 12 years. He blamed the company's decline on increased foreign competition and a dramatic and sustained drop in the demand for plants. Many estates with gardens had been forced to close down, which reduced his market.

In closing proceedings, the Official Receiver observed that, 'he personally held the highest opinion of Messrs Kelway's business, and he hoped he had not depreciated its value. It was an old-established firm of repute, and to the right purchaser would be a valuable asset'. He further commented that the whole affair was 'rather tragic'. James Kelway was duly declared bankrupt.

Less than a month later, however, the local newspaper reported with evident relief that the company had been purchased by a local syndicate and would resume trading under the new name of Kelway and Son (1933) Limited. Moreover, James Kelway was to be retained as the manager of the new company, under the managing director, John Owen Lloyd.

The bankruptcy order was discharged on 14 March 1935, and James continued to manage the company. Even with reduced resources during the Depression, by the end of the 1930s it had offices in London and Toronto.

The end of an era
The Second World War was another period of great difficulty for Kelways. Their resources had been weakened by the legacy of the earlier war, and the contraction of the nursery business during the economic depression of the 1930s had never allowed them to return to the worldwide successes of their heyday. The preface to their catalogue for 1940 repeated the pleas that had become all too familiar during the First World War.

> 'In addition to our war-time activities in using the greater part of our nursery land for the growing of food supplies, we rely upon valued old and new customers to help us to make the best use of our large and valuable stocks of perennial plants, shrubs and bulbs, which have taken so many years and so much labour to produce, by sending us their orders however small.'

Four long years later they reprinted a quote from a customer which must have struck a chord: 'A thousand thanks for the lovely plants. The old song says "There will always be an England". My best wish is that there will always be a Kelways at Langport'.

During the war Kelways had turned to food production, keeping only a nucleus stock of each flower. John Owen Lloyd served as a Somerset District Officer for the Ministry of Agriculture, from 1940 until 1947, when he returned to the business full-time and began to rebuild stocks of the firm's specialities. He had also acquired a reputation for breeding Friesian cattle, which conveniently provided manure for the nursery.

John Owen Lloyd

James Kelway had remained as managing director of the company since 1933, and his foreword to the gladioli and seed catalogue for 1950/51 showed how much the association meant to him.

'On the eve of the one hundredth year since the first Kelway founded the firm his grandson is grateful for the opportunity to express his very sincere appreciation, not only of the patronage which has supported the firm in years long past, but of the continuation of that confidence shown by so many descendants of old clients, and by the many fresh customers of recent years, due to their recommendation. He is proud to be still associated with Kelway and Son and in so honourable a field of horticulture, and to be able on behalf of the firm to assure all of its determination and ability to give their orders the best possible care and attention.'

Less than two years later, in August 1952, he died, which marked the end of the Kelway family's involvement with the nursery. It is said that on his death his office was locked, and never used again.

Kelways' 1949 catalogue marked 'JK', showing the peony named after his grandfather

Chapter 3
Plants and propagation

It is striking, on looking back at the history of Kelways nursery, how versatile they were. Although they were to become famous for gladioli and peonies, their drive to produce improved varieties of all sorts of plants led to a depth of interest in many different areas that is quite remarkable. Between 1859 and 1893 Kelways were awarded certificates of merit by the Floral Committee of the RHS for 12 different flowers and one fern.

The first James Kelway had started his professional career in charge of remodelling the gardens at Dillington House. This allowed him to manage extensive areas of borders, kitchen gardens and large greenhouses, in order to supply the house with fruit, vegetables and flowers. It was while he was here that he developed his interest in hybridising.

A visit to Kelways by contributors to the *Gardeners' Magazine* in 1892 noted that, 'In addition to the fruit and vegetable departments, the specialities grown are amaryllids, paeonies, cannas, gladioli, delphiniums, pyrethrums, gaillardias, and herbaceous plants, the latter collection being very large, and worth a long journey to see.'
A great deal of the success of the business depended on introducing new varieties each year; exhibiting them at prestigious horticultural shows, and using the medals and prizes they won as evidence of the quality of their products. Their reputation was founded on the sheer scale of their activity, and the simple but crucial fact that they had grown and trialled their plants themselves. In 1913 they stated, 'we have over 300 acres of our own land under cultivation for stock selection and small crops; and … thousands of acres planted for us in that and other localities by expert growers from our Langport grown seeds.'

In the early 20th century the leading British gardening journal, writing of the 'famous hybridists', stated: 'That great leader, Kelway, of Langport, has enriched English gardens with a hundred noble flowers – delphiniums, paeonies, gladioli, and other plants precious to the gardener'.

Propagation was clearly one of their main interests, and a primary source of income. James's son William recounted how he had propagated six hundred plants of his new dahlia 'Baron Taunton' in one spring, which 'sold freely at 10/6 a plant'. It also won the Silver Cup at the first ever Langport Flower Show that year, 1859.

Successful plant breeding also demanded a long term strategy. William noted that it took twenty years after cross-fertilisation took place to build up sufficient stock to go into production. However, in terms of peonies, 'we have so many years practising at the Art that we are actually putting into commerce year after year 25 new varieties'.

Gladioli
James Kelway always said that it was his discovery of the beauty of the gladiolus that fuelled his interest in the cultivation of plants. He was quick to establish a reputation as a first class specialist in gladioli: 'the Souchet of England', as one writer described him. Eugene Souchet was the Head Gardener at the Palace of Fontainebleau. He had won first prize for his gladioli at the Paris International Exhibition of 1867, and was acknowledged as the world's foremost grower of gladioli. James had met him at Fontainebleau in 1874, and they became friends.

James distributed the first of the modern florists' hybrid gladioli in the 1860s. By the 1870s their gladiolus catalogues listed almost 800 varieties. At that time they had

8 acres devoted to gladioli: 6 for plants in bloom and 2 for seedlings.

James's diaries reveal the scale and complexity of his meticulous approach. On Saturday 4 March 1876, they 'finished sorting and naming all the gladioli, 2,717 sorts. I put them in order for planting. First this year's spawn put away in pots of fine soil...Second last year's spawn to be sown in beds as soon as the location permits. Third small bulbs of the size of peas to be sown in beds. Fourth bulbs the size of a coalnut to be sown in July in beds and fifth large bulbs to be planted ...for blooming...each of these sets making 5 times 2,700.'

In 1878 a *Gardeners' Chronicle* article began, 'Mr Kelway's name has been long associated with this flower, and few, if any, have done so much to improve it.' They reported that Kelways were sending out from 3-4,000 cut flower spikes a week during the flowering season.

Gladioli spikes packed in boxes

James Kelway addressed the Royal Horticultural Society on the subject of the cultivation of gladioli in September 1890. In 1899, the year of James' death, Kelways could claim that their 25 acres of gladioli constituted the largest culture of its kind in the world.

The early 20th century saw the development of an entirely new strain of gladioli, the 'Lang-Prims', as they were called – the name being an amalgamation of 'Langport' and 'primulinus'. In 1903 they received *Gladiolus primulinus* from Francis Fox, who was part of the firm of consulting engineers then engaged in building the Victoria Falls Bridge over the River Zambezi.

Lang-prim gladioli

Fox exhibited them at the RHS Show in August 1904, where they excited considerable interest. Kelways crossed them with their own *Gladiolus Kelwayi* variety to produce a completely new strain, which was greatly admired. 'One of the greatest horticultural triumphs of this century', was how one writer described them.

In 1908, the *Gardeners' Magazine* wrote that, 'in the improvement of gladioli, and the creation of new forms, the greatest credit belongs to Messrs Kelway and Son, Langport, Somerset, who for about half a century have worked wonders with these flowers, and raised them to their present high position in the garden.'

BUTTERFLY and MINIATURE COLLECTION

PETER PAN	ARES	MELODIE
STATUETTE	BOSTON	BO PEEP

3 of each 15/-; 6 of each 29/-; 12 of each 56/-

The above collection was grown and photographed at our Langport Nurseries

A collection of gladioli in 1956

38

The younger James Kelway was responsible for introducing a new scented gladiolus into this country. In 1925 Captain Erskine, British Representative at Gore, in Abyssinia, sent him some corms which he flowered in his own garden. James wanted to name the new flower *erskini*, but Captain Erskine preferred it to be named after his wife, and so it became known as *Gladiolus murieliae*. In 1932 the British Gladiolus Society gave it an Award of Merit, although some time later it was reclassified as *Acidanthera bicolour murieliae*.

In 1927, they were able to mount a display in the British Gladiolus Society's annual exhibition of no less than 3,000 gladioli blooms in 125 varieties. They were rewarded by the award of the only gold medal for best exhibit, as well as other prizes.

By the 1930s, however, they could not compete with gladioli produced abroad. An interview with the *Daily Mail* in 1931 quoted James: 'We can raise the most beautiful gladioli in the world and we can grow them very well indeed, but we are up against competition from foreigners. We could quickly employ double the number of hands if people would buy at home'.

Peonies
James Kelway first tried to improve the peony in 1864, using *P. officinalis* and *P. corallina* (now known as *P. mascula*). His son William, in a letter to George Paul dated 6 June 1890, says that *P. corallina* had been collected by his father James' sister, from Steep Holm, an island in the Bristol Channel.

Twenty years later their catalogue listed 250 varieties, 104 of which were Kelways' new introductions. They helped spread the popularity of peonies to the USA by exporting crowns and offering prize medals at large flower shows in New York and Boston.

The artist Monet was said to have ordered peonies from Kelways for his garden at Giverny, though the catalogue of the Royal Academy exhibition in 1990, 'Monet in the 90s', suggests that Monet obtained seed from Kelways rather than plants. 'He attended the horticultural shows in Paris and ordered seeds from specialist foreign, as well as French, merchants. One of these, Kelway & Son, The Royal Seed and Nursery Establishment in Langport, Somerset, had won a gold medal at the Paris International Exhibition of 1889'.

The younger James Kelway in 1931 with the peony
Kelway's Glorious

In an interview with *The Garden* in 1900, William recalled how his enthusiasm for peonies had been sparked by the sight of 'the lads and maidens of the countryside bedecked with the fine old *Paeonia officinalis* at a village wake, and he determined at once to procure as many species as possible from all parts of the world to raise up a new and glorious race.'

Promoting peonies in 1901

The younger James Kelway took a special interest in peonies and greatly expanded the breeding programme. In 1910 there were about 20 acres of peonies, five of which were under fruit trees.

The development of improved varieties of peony took many years. James Kelway described the process in a 1929 article.

'We keep the seed in soil for a year before sowing to soften the hard covering. Then it takes four or five years before we can judge the flower, and to make a small stock another four or five seasons. It is frequently fifteen or twenty years before a seedling makes its first appearance in a catalogue, and so the cost of production is high.'

As the 20th century wore on, peonies gradually eclipsed gladioli as Kelways' trademark product. Peonies became fashionable, and Kelways claimed the credit, with some justification.

Criticisms were voiced from time to time. In 1928 the American Peony Society paid them a rather back-handed compliment: 'The firm of Kelway & Son, in England, in spite of their notorious carelessness in the matter of names, must always be given credit for having originated some of the finest peonies that have come from any source... enough to atone for a multitude of errors.' They were more enthusiastic in 1942, when they conducted a poll of their members as to which was the 'most magnificent peony', and *Kelway's Glorious* topped the list.

When Vita Sackville-West was writing about peonies in 1949, the firm she mentioned was Kelways. Of the varieties she recommended, two were white: *Kelways Glorious*, at 12s 6d 'is a fine white', *Duchesse de Nemours*, at 5s 'is white with a slightly yellowish tinge and smaller flowers'. Note that the Kelway's variety was over twice the price!

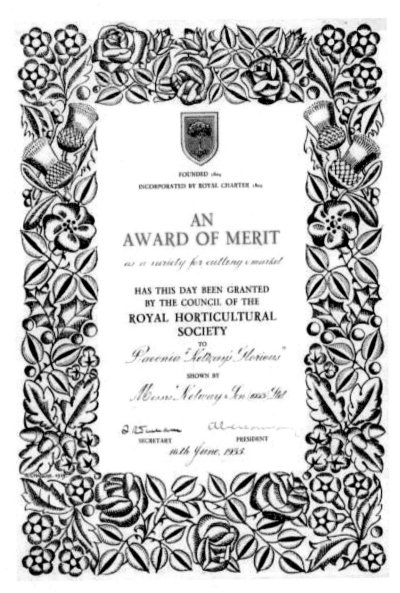

RHS Award of Merit to Kelway's Glorious, 1935

Advertisement in a 1930s Somerset tourist brochure

44

Peony Valley

Peonies were – and still are – grown in a valley at Barrymore Farm. It quickly became known as Peony Valley. An excursion, by car or train, to see Kelways' peonies in full bloom became a popular pastime in the 1920s and 1930s. A temporary railway station called Peony Halt was said to have been set up near Peony Valley to let passengers alight close to their destination.

Marion Cran, a well-known writer and radio broadcaster on gardening subjects, was completely bowled over by her Peony Valley experience.

> 'Mr. James Kelway took me to see the flowers in person – a signal honour which I fear I roundly abused; lingering bewildered, intoxicated with sheer beauty, longing for nothing but to stay for ever in the enchanted vale and learn by heart each matchless bloom'.

Peony Valley in full bloom c.1930

She also extolled the virtues of Peony Valley in a radio broadcast in 1928, saying, 'No one can go and come back

45

just the same as they went in; that valley makes you love paeonies. Those who suffer from paeony-passion as I do have fallen in love with them'.

Delphiniums

Victor Lemoine, a French nurseryman, and James Kelway are acknowledged as the 'fathers' of many of the modern delphinium cultivars. James imported some of Lemoine's hybrids and began to develop his own varieties. They were based on the small-flowered *elatum* types, but with bigger flowers and spikes. One of his most successful was a blue and plum semi-double called *King of Delphiniums*. His keen eye for novelty picked out what was to become an astonishing new strain of white delphiniums. *Beauty of Langport*, introduced in 1887, was a startling creamy white, and *Primrose* had a bright yellow 'eye'.

New delphiniums advertised in 1913

46

Visitors from the *Gardeners' Magazine* in 1892 were very impressed. 'Inexorable lapse of time pointed to our return train, and we left Langport with pleasant recollections of a day made enjoyable by the kindness of the members of the firm and their foremen, and with a lasting impression of the finest delphiniums in the horticultural world.' Delphiniums were grown on about 10 acres, and the *Journal of Horticulture* reported that Kelways had 200,000 in stock.

One writer noted that of the 32 new varieties of delphinium honoured by the RHS up to 1899, 28 were raised at Langport. When the RHS published its *Tentative checklist of delphinium names* in 1949, Kelways were credited with introducing 22% of the 2,540 varieties listed, almost all of which they had bred themselves. Lemoine's introductions comprised only 12%, and Blackmore & Langdon's, 7% of the total.

Irises
Kelways had always cultivated irises, but after the Second World War they took a major step forward by buying the entire collection of the Award Iris Nurseries of Barnet, Hertfordshire. They issued their first iris catalogue in 1950, and from then on irises became a frequent feature of their medal-winning displays.

In 1976 Kelways unveiled a ground-breaking new strain of May-flowering intermediate mid-height iris, a cross between tall bearded iris and dwarf irises. They offered no less than 50 varieties, all called names beginning 'Langport', from *Langport Carnival* to *Langport Wren*, and dated between 1968 and 1973. *Langport Wren* has an RHS Award of Garden Merit.

Intermediate irises on the cover of the 1976/77 catalogue

Pyrethrums

Pyrethrums were another success story for their plant breeding techniques. They had been introducing new varieties of both single and double flowers since the 1880s. Between 1859 and 1892 the RHS Floral Committee awarded 23 certificates for different varieties of pyrethrums – all but two were won by Kelways, and 12 of those were First Class Certificates.

Kelways still hold an RHS Award of Garden Merit for the pyrethrum 'James Kelway' (*Tanacetum coccineum*). 'Langport Scarlet', which was given an Award of Merit in

1908, was said to be an improvement on 'James Kelway'.

Pyrethrum 'Langport Scarlet'

Hollyhocks
In the 1880s, to their evident delight, Kelways beat Lord Hawke's display of new hollyhocks to win the prize that Hawke himself had put up at the Crystal Palace Show. Lord Hawke's complaints to the newspapers that Kelways' variety was too similar to another went unheeded.

By 1904 they were able to say, with some magnanimity, 'As far back as the fifties, Kelway & Son, with the late Lord Hawke and one or two other growers, were the chief and most successful cultivators and exhibitors of the Hollyhock.'

Cineraria
In 1895 a debate arose about the origin of the cultivated cineraria. The elder James Kelway himself wrote to the *Gardeners' Magazine* to assert his claim that the florists' cineraria had originated with him, from sports he had grown

in 1837, while he was Head Gardener at Dillington House, and before he had set up in his own business. He had given some of these improved seedlings to Webber & Pearce, nurserymen of nearby Merriott, who had in turn distributed them to their customers, causing the confusion about their origin. This seemed to settle the matter, and it is now generally accepted that the modern cineraria has developed from James Kelway's improvement of *Cineraria cruenta.*

Sweet peas
At the turn of the last century, in 1901, Kelways were offering no less than 97 different varieties of sweet peas. In 1913 their *Manual of horticulture* boasted that they had 10 acres of sweet peas under cultivation for seed. By 1941 they were only advertising 24 varieties, and in their centenary year, 1951, only 16.

Cover for a collection of sweet peas

Vegetables and fruit
Kelways also specialised in the cultivation of new strains of cucumber, claiming to be pioneers in the introduction of improved varieties: 'Many of the finest varieties in commerce *originated in our houses*'. They marketed 'Kelway's Victory'

in the 1850s, which James had developed in 1843, before he founded his nursery business.

James Kelway tending his cucumbers

In a sign of the times, and a rather poignant portent of their shrinking market, in 1897 they also offered collections of vegetable seeds. 'These collections are useful to amateurs who do not employ a regular gardener; it enables them to order a complete collection for the whole year's supply without the trouble of writing an order in detail'.

Given that pears feature in the Kelway coat of arms, it is perhaps surprising that they were not more interested in them. But in 1904 one appears. They advertised a 'fine new pear, 'Kelway's King', developed by William, a cross between *Glou Morceau* and *Marie Louise.'*

Kelways introduced the Japanese wineberry to Britain as an ornamental fruit. The RHS Floral Committee awarded it a First Class Certificate in 1892. In 1901 Kelways assured customers of its hardiness. 'It bears abundance of fruit at

Langport in the open field, exposed to every change of weather.'

A whimsical illustration of 'Kelway's Monstrous' leek

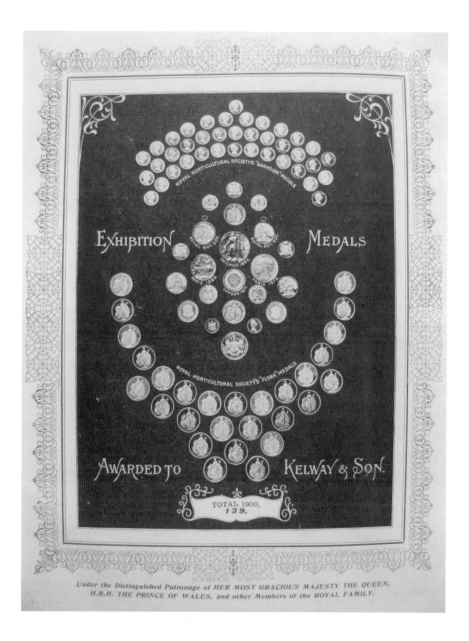

A typical format for advertising their past successes

Chapter 4
Marketing and promotion

Kelways have always had a flair for self-promotion. From their earliest days in business they worked hard to maximise their assets and to seek out ingenious ways of marketing their products. Even when using traditional methods, such as press advertisements, the terms in which they presented themselves are florid and exuberant, reflecting perhaps the often gaudy flowers that were to become their trademark.

One of the most reliable and effective ways of getting their plants noticed was to enter horticultural shows, and preferably to win top prizes. Awards were used to promote winning varieties, which could then be sold at a premium price the following year.

'Royal' Kelways
In the earliest catalogue in Kelways' possession, dated Spring 1872, they describe themselves as 'The Royal Nurseries'. The cover proudly states: 'Patronized by Her Most Gracious Majesty Queen Victoria and His Royal Highness the Prince of Wales'. For many years, they used variations on the 'royal' theme, including 'The Royal Seed and Nursery Establishment' and 'The Royal Horticulturists'.

In making this a feature of their publicity it seems that they were skating on thin ice. There is no evidence that Kelways have ever held a Royal Warrant.

From time to time they sent seeds, plants or cut flowers to the Royal Household. Whether this was unsolicited or by request or order is not clear. In 1896 they sent 'a box of flowers of our new Herbaceous Paeonies with a descriptive statement as their culture at Langport, both of which we were allowed by special permission to present to our

54

Gracious Sovereign'. Finally, they were rewarded with a reply from the Private Secretary to Queen Victoria, which thanked them for sending 'the beautiful specimen flowers ... for Her Majesty's inspection'.

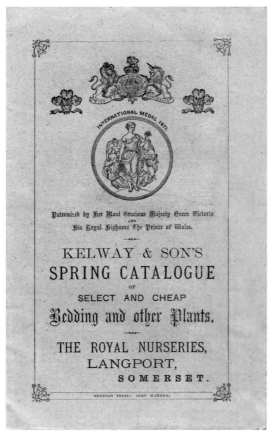

Kelway's catalogue for 1872

They seem to have got cold feet about using the 'royal' word after 1928, when it suddenly disappears and is replaced by 'The hardy plant nurseries'. After the firm was taken over in 1933, the 'Royal Nurseries' tag came back into use, and there it remained until it disappeared for good in 1994.

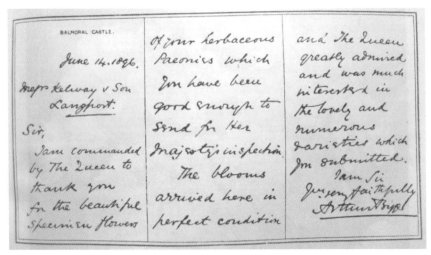

A treasured letter of thanks from Balmoral

Catalogues and manuals

The large and lavishly illustrated manuals of horticulture first published by Kelways in the 1890s were much, much more than mere catalogues. By the first decade of the twentieth century they ran to over 300 pages, most of them illustrated. They included articles reprinted from other sources; pages of testimonials; lists of their medals and prizes; extensive horticultural notes and growing advice, and a wide range of offers, collections, competitions and gardening sundries. In short, they were used to market and further enhance the Kelway reputation as the pre-eminent nursery and seedsmen of the time.

Wherever possible they used the writings of famous gardeners, such as William Robinson and Gertrude Jekyll, suggesting that well-respected horticulturists shared their approach to planting and indeed might have endorsed their products.

Gertrude Jekyll is said to have been a close friend of the younger James Kelway, staying with him at Wearne Wyche from time to time – possibly while she was working on Hestercombe Gardens, in Taunton. She wrote a foreword to *Gardens of Delight*, a supplement to Kelways' Manual for 1909, praising their 'long-sustained effort and unwearied patience' and admiring 'the wealth of splendid flowers in all the best classes of hardy plants for which these renowned gardens are justly famous'.

Kelway's catalogue for 1893

Some wholesale seed catalogues appeared in editions targeted at other countries. In 1918 there was a 'Colonial edition'; in 1923 a Canadian one. In 1932 and 1934 they issued a 'US Edition', whose prices were in dollars and cents, although later ones in 1937 and 1938 reverted to sterling prices. An 'Empire edition' appeared in 1935, for Australia, New Zealand, South Africa, and India, but these foreign editions are rarities.

Illustrations

The early manuals were illustrated by line drawings and reproductions of paintings, some of which were specially commissioned, whereas others were obviously 'discovered' and then exploited for publicity purposes. The 1895 Manual, for example, included a reproduction of a painting of peonies by W J Muckley, which had been exhibited at the Royal Academy in 1892. 'This picture of tree paeonies, after plants supplied by us, is from the brush of one of our customers, the well-known artist, W J Muckley, Esq, Loweswater Hall, Cockermouth, who very kindly gave us permission to publish a reproduction.'

Two attractive Marsh Lambert illustrations

The drawings themselves are of particular note. One of the best known artists they used was H C Marsh Lambert, a children's book illustrator, whose simple depictions expressed a childlike joy in the flowers she drew.

Kelways were pioneers in the use of three-colour process blocks to produce illustrations. They printed their first colour photograph in the Manual for 1900, of the delphinium, 'Duke of Connaught'. No doubt with an eye to greater circulation, they added a suggestion along the inner edge of the page: 'for framing please cut along this line'.

Kelway borders
For many years Kelways had been offering collections of hardy perennial border plants, 'to save amateurs the time and trouble in choosing for themselves'. Their list of 'selections' began with the simple 'Border selection for beauty in the garden'.

This was the idea which, by the end of the century, seemed to develop into 'Kelway's artistic borders', which were recreations of 'living paintings'. They were careful to emphasize the difference between the selections and the artistic borders, which were an altogether more sophisticated – and considerably more expensive – concept. They came complete with suggested planting plans, carefully itemised with names, colours and measurements.

This development capitalised on the fashionable move away from 'carpet bedding' and towards a more informal style of massed planting. An article in the *Gardeners' Magazine* in 1910, reporting on a visit to the Langport nursery, remarked on the 'fine example of a colour-scheme border, which, as everyone knows, Messrs. Kelway have made a special study … A Kelway border, seen at any time from March to October, is a mass of beautifully-mingled colours, bold and striking in effect.'

A Kelway colour border

To further promote their borders, they published *Gardens of Delight*, which was a lavishly illustrated advertisement for the Kelway approach to gardening. It first appeared as a supplement to their *Manual of horticulture* for 1909, but the revised edition that was published in 1914 was a magnificent work. It consists of 52 pages, each edged with a coloured border of flowers and leaves, arranged in the form of a scrapbook. It contains a mixture of advice, extracts from other sources, quotations and observations.

The work includes many photographs, some in colour, all designed to show Kelway borders to best advantage. It is arguably James's finest work.

Gardens of Delight, published in 1914

Kelway Medals

Not content with winning awards themselves, in the early 1890s Kelways donated awards of their own to the Royal Horticultural Society. The James Kelway Medal was to be awarded for gladioli.

THE KELWAY — GLADIOLUS MEDAL.

(Won in 1890 by the Rt. Hon. LORD WIMBORNE, Canford Manor, Dorset ; Mr. Crasp, Gardener.
Won in 1893 by JNO. C. FORDY, Esq., Warkworth, Northumberland.)

The James Kelway Medal

The William Kelway Medal, however, was more wide-ranging: 'in order to extend the cultivation of improved forms of some of the most beautiful flowers which can be grown in the gardens of the United Kingdom…to be awarded for paeonies, pyrethrums, delphiniums and gaillardias'.

When the RHS decided to stop the practice of allowing different types of awards and medals to proliferate, and politely told Kelways that their medals were no longer required, Kelways offered them instead to other horticultural shows, both in the UK and abroad.

Perfume

Inspired by the popularity of Peony Valley, their 'show field' of peony varieties, Kelways even developed a peony perfume. They claimed that experts had described the scent as 'one of absolute individuality and distinction, not overpowering, but with just that delicacy of fragrance that is found only in the Paeony Valley.'

It made its first appearance in their 1938 catalogue of hardy perennials, but sadly it was to be a short-lived initiative. Wartime regulations meant that they had to switch to producing a peony-scented talcum powder, which hardly had the same impact. It made its last appearance in a 1950 catalogue, and has not been repeated. It was a rare marketing disappointment.

The range of Peony Valley perfumes

Chapter 5
Shows and prizes

The founder of the firm, James Kelway, had a reputation for liking competitions. His son said of him that he 'was very fond of competing for prizes, and of who may well be said never knew when he was beaten.' The ability to exhibit new varieties of all sorts of plants year after year, and win prizes for them, formed the foundation of Kelways' reputation.

The *Gardeners' Chronicle* recognised this in an article in 1972: '… the name of Kelway & Son Ltd … is pre-eminent in what is a highly competitive field. They are one of the few firms who exhibit at shows in all parts of the country, collecting gold medals wherever they go.'

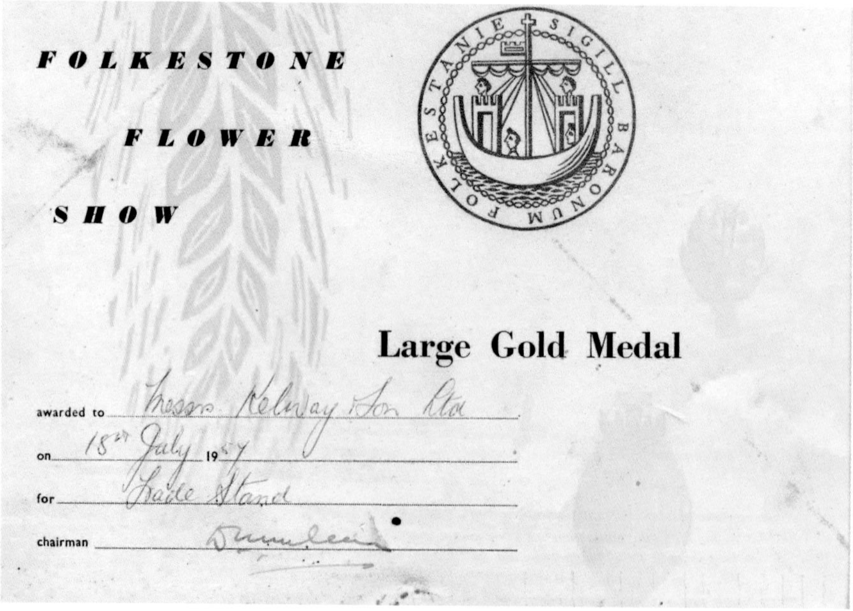

FOLKESTONE

FLOWER

SHOW

Large Gold Medal

awarded to _Messrs Kelway & Son Ltd_

on _18th July 19_

for _Trade Stand_

chairman

A far-flung venue yields a gold medal

Exhibiting at horticultural and agricultural shows must have demanded considerable resources. Many shows were staged over more than one day, and some shows took place simultaneously. Kelways were regular exhibitors at shows in London, particularly those organised by the RHS. They also took part in exhibitions abroad, particularly in Paris and in the USA.

A list of shows in 1930 at which medals were won reveals 17 different shows, at venues ranging from York to Liskeard. By 1936 this had risen to 40, from Melrose to Bournemouth. After the Second World War their operations were scaled back slightly. A show card issued in 1950 predicts 31 proposed show dates from April to October. Most of them were two-day shows, and 14 of the 31 were in London. Fifty years later, the changed nature of horticultural business was reflected in the number of shows Kelways attended in 2000 – only eight. In 2011, their 160th year, they will attend four: Cardiff, Malvern, Chelsea, and Gardeners' World Live.

Staff preparing flowers for a London show c. 1899

Kelways at Chelsea

Since its establishment in 1913, the RHS Chelsea Show has been staged a total of 89 times. Kelways have only missed 10 shows, 8 of which were during the period before the firm's change of ownership in 1933. There have only been 7 occasions when they have mounted an exhibit that has failed to win an award. Since 1936 they have won an award at every show they've attended, and in some years they mounted 3 different exhibits and won a medal for each of them.

Kelways were exhibitors at the first Chelsea Show in May 1913, where they won a Silver-Gilt Banksian Medal for 'herbaceous flowers'. They are one of the few original participants still exhibiting today. For the first four years they took out full page advertisements inside the front cover of the Show catalogue. They are full colour plates of individual flowers, including: *Gladiolus Richard Martin* and *Delphinium persicum*.

In the early years of the shows their exhibits are given general descriptions, such as 'hardy herbaceous plants', but since 1930 they have been more detailed. Not surprisingly, peonies have featured in all of their exhibits, with the sole exception of 1947, when only tulips were mentioned. Irises and tree peonies also make frequent appearances, as well as tulips and pyrethrums.

Kelways won their first Chelsea Gold Medal in 1976, for an exhibit of peonies. To date they have won no less than 15 gold medals at Chelsea, all of which have been awarded for peonies or irises, or both. In all Kelways have taken home a total of 125 Chelsea medals of one level or another - an impressive haul.

The Queen Mother

KELWAYS

Chelsea Show - 1961

Royal Lodge Windsor

KELWAY'S PAEONIES
June Flowering

A royal order at Chelsea in 1961

Chapter 6
Kelways after the Kelways

John Lloyd, son of John Owen Lloyd, joined the firm in 1958. He bought the company from his father in 1974 and leased additional land from him. A quiet, unassuming man, he was passionate about daffodils.

John Lloyd and his sister Sheila with Kelway's Lovely peonies at the Chelsea Flower Show in 1961

In the late 1980s personal circumstances forced him to sell the business. Australians Barry and Beatrice Moignard purchased it in 1990 and moved the centre of operations from the original Kelways buildings on the Somerton Road half a mile up the road to Barrymore Farm. Barry Moignard tried to revitalise the business and capitalise on its rich heritage. Peony Valley re-opened on 15 June 1991 after having been closed to the public for 50 years.

Sadly, his ambitious strategy failed to produce results, and at the end of 1992 he handed over as managing director to

John Landell Mills, a garden consultant. Mills pursued an aggressive marketing strategy which was intended to re-establish Kelways' national and international reputation, but unfortunately this too failed to put the business on a sound footing.

The receivers were called in again in November 1993, and 28 of the 35 staff were made redundant.

The Receiver arranged for the Somerton Road buildings to be bought by South Somerset District Council under a Compulsory Purchase Order to prevent them from deteriorating any further. Following a two-day enquiry held at the Langport Arms Hotel in April 1994, one scheme to convert the buildings into 23 homes was rejected by the planning inspector because it would alter the historical appearance of Kelways and also change Langport's rural character. He said: 'No other Victorian Nursery development of this size has survived to this day to anything like the same extent. I therefore regard it as of particular importance'. The CPO was given the go-ahead, and in August 1995, SSDC approved the development of the site by the new owners, Grosvenor Place Holdings.

The nursery business itself was rescued by Chris and Liz Johnson, of McBean's Orchids. Kelways was at its lowest ebb. The peonies from Peony Valley were in crates under the fir trees, and the company records were stacked in an open sided barn. Chris Johnson's quiet, measured approach to rebuilding the business bore fruit, and gradually it restored its reputation with its customers and with the Royal Horticultural Society.

When Chris retired in 2008, Dave Root, who had joined the company in 1993, took over ownership of the nursery and became its managing director.

Kelways today

Although they no longer have a plant breeding programme, Kelways are said to have introduced more peonies than any other British nursery and perhaps more than any nursery in the world. At the Chelsea Flower Show in 2009 they had a new tree peony, *Paeonia suffruticosa* 'Shintenchi', sourced by a friend who searches Japan for new specimens.

The nursery now extends to 40 acres, of which 6 are devoted to peonies. They grow about 500 varieties, of which about 300 are probably not grown anywhere else, and they hold the National Collection of pre-1940 peonies. There are nearly 30 varieties still on sale which bear the Kelway name, and Peony Valley still displays hundreds of historic varieties.

The business has three main branches: the retail plant centre, the mail order side, and contract plant growing. The search for new markets for their specialist products is central to their survival.

The nursery entrance today

Plans for the future include opening a coffee shop at the plant centre, developing Peony Valley into a show garden, and planning a heritage area to display some of the historical catalogues and artefacts that bring Kelways' history to life.

Over the history of the nursery each generation of owners has brought their own interests. Dave Root is introducing a wide range of ferns to add to the list of Kelways' specialities.

A final word

Kelways is more than just a name; it represents the glorious spirit of rural Britain – the innovation, the enterprise, and the endurance of a small family business which became an international legend. Let's echo that wartime correspondent: 'My best wish is that there will always be a Kelways at Langport'.

Index